21st Century Communities

A Youth Inquiry Project

Foreword by the Hon. Scott Brison PC, MP
Edited by Steven Van Zoost, PhD

Order this book online at all major book sellers.
ISBN 978-1-257-91406-7

Edited by Steven Van Zoost, PhD

A first edition (2010) was published by Learning for a Cause Publications in Montreal.
Library and Archives Canada Cataloging in Publication Data Available at:
www.collectionscanada.ca/amicus/index-e.html
ISBN: 978-0-9812071-5-5

10 9 8 7 6 5 4 3 2 1

Contents

Dedication

This book is dedicated to young people who make a positive difference in their communities and to those who support them.

Foreword

Frequently, I hear politicians decry the apathy of today's youth. They refer to the fact that in the last federal election only twenty percent of those citizens eligible to vote for the first time actually voted. I argue that young people are not apathetic and are in fact interested in issues and ideas. The reason why young people are rejecting politics is that politics seems less and less about ideas and more about tribal warfare. The thought-provoking and challenging essays in this anthology affirm my view.

Communities sustain, support, and define us. I grew up in Cheverie. My family have lived "down the shore" for generations. When I lived away (first, as a student at Dalhousie University, and then in New York in my twenties as I pursued my business career), I longed for home—for my community. Our collective yearning for community is so strong, that even in a big city such as New York, people self-organized into smaller communities defined by interests—attesting to the diverse definition of community that this collection of essays provides.

I've come to believe that communities are stronger when united by purpose. In rural Nova Scotia, volunteer fire fighters not only risk their lives to save others, but spend countless hours training and raising money. Church suppers and community breakfasts not only raise money to sustain vital organizations, but they bring friends, neighbours, and families together to share food and fellowship.

In our closely knit rural communities when one family faces a challenge, the community unites behind them to share the burden. Regardless of the crisis, no family faces the challenge alone. Whether it's a child who needs unaffordable surgery or when an uninsured home burns, community efforts self-organize instinctively out of a sense of duty and purpose. Communities are united when they have a sense of purpose. Communities without a sense of purpose, tend to drift apart.

As an M.P. representing rural and small town Nova Scotia, I am inspired by the resilience, determination, and selflessness of community builders. I have tremendous respect for the small business owners, volunteer fire fighters, church stewards, hockey coaches, and service club leaders who work tirelessly to keep our communities alive. I am also inspired by our youth, who in this volume discuss the nature and importance that community plays in all of our lives, from the Albertan First Nations community of Fort McKay, to the town of Windsor, Nova Scotia.

The following essays explore communities in terms of culture, education, faith, industry, tradition, prejudice, poverty, sustainability, and technology. In addition to the contributors' penetrating insights, these essays reveal that young people are not disaffected, but are indeed interested and engaged in a wide range of issues and ideas. These essays not only reflect that young people see the importance of community, but that they have begun to think of themselves as potential community builders, and perhaps even nation builders.

Hon. Scott Brison PC, MP
www.brison.ca

Introduction

At first glance, this anthology may look like a collection of essays. Well, it is. Essays allow us to articulate our observations and thinking about the world. However, I prefer to think of this anthology not as a collection of essays, but as a collection of thinking projects where young people raise questions that they consider important for their own life and for the lives of others.

The thinking projects in this anthology were written by students in my Advanced English 12 class in January, 2010. In the last three weeks of our course, we explored what defines a community in the 21st century. I should set the record straight: this topic was not my idea. This topic emerged as a way of connecting the diverse interests of the students enrolled in the course and we created a label to describe our endeavour—a "Youth Inquiry Project."

Each writer had an individualized inquiry question that shaped their thinking about communities. These inquiry questions guided students' observations about their own communities in rural Nova Scotia as well as their observations of a contrasting community in northern Alberta, the First Nations community of Fort McKay. On page x, an alternative table of contents is offered that lists the inquiry questions that guided the writing of each chapter.

Beyond engaging students in thinking projects, this anthology also illustrates students' writing projects. As a high school teacher, I notice that the persuasive essay is a dominant structure in students' writing. The essays in this collection are intended to model how high school students can use a range of essay structures to express their ideas. On page xi, an alternative table of contents is offered to show how the essays reflect a variety of structures: cause and effect, classification, pros/cons, definition, expository, explanation/informative, personal, persuasive, and narrative essays. This anthology does not explicitly teach the merits of each of these structures as such information is readily available in other high school resources. However, most of our high school texts do not feature student writing samples that are inclusive of students' writing strengths and struggles.

As an editor, I have been careful not to intrude heavily on students' ideas or stylistic choices. This provides a collection of work that reflects what high school students are able to produce. You, gentle reader, may have additional ideas to support the writers' thoughts and writing choices. I encourage you to use these essays to reflect on writing strategies. I should also point-out that as a writing project, the authors have included footnotes about the craft of writing. These annotations provide insight into to the writer's intentions and are useful in understanding how writers deploy specific writing techniques in consideration of an essay's structure.

The purpose of this anthology is to engage students in thinking and writing projects, and to engage teachers in thinking about pedagogical projects. Following the students' chapters, I offer a teacher-reflection about working with individualized inquiry questions in designing a classroom program. While this reflection is intended for educators, many high school students appreciate when I make my methodological stances explicit.

Throughout this Youth Inquiry Project, I have watched students be deeply committed to learning and I have experienced how students can foster and value community within my classroom. This anthology is a testament to the learning that is possible when young people become participants in making curricular decisions that are meaningful to their current and future lives. I hope that this anthology will spread the optimism that I have about working with young people in our schools and communities. While some might consider high school as a place to prepare young people for their future lives, I am proud of my students for who they are now.

Steven Van Zoost, PhD
www.stevenvanzoost.com

Additional Resources

The students involved in this Youth Inquiry Project are also featured in the following resources:

Documentaries

Van Zoost, S., Armour, D., & Gibson, P. (Producers). (2010). *Questions to Learn: A Youth Inquiry Project* [motion picture]. Canada: Avon View High School. Available at www.stevenvanzoost.com

Nova Scotia Department of Education, Learning Resources and Technology (Producer). (2009). *Create!: Get inspired by the Arts in Our Schools* [motion picture]. Available at http://www.ednet.ns.ca/create-dvd.shtml

Journal Article

Van Zoost, S. (2010, Winter). So there I was… on a Métis trapline. *Aviso*, pp. 30-31.

Book Chapter

Van Zoost, S. (2011). Impact on Engagement: Place-Based Learning [a case study]. In K. Hume *Tuned Out: Engaging the 21st Century Learner.* Don Mills, ON: Pearson Canada, p. 151.

Keynote Address

Van Zoost, S. (2009). *21st Century Literacies and Learners in Nova Scotia*: Literacy Success 10-12 Implementation, NS Dept. of Education.

University Courses

These students' classroom work beyond the scope of this book was featured in fifteen Masters of Education courses for Mount Saint Vincent University and St. Francis Xavier University taught in Halifax, North Sydney, St. John's, Gander, Corner Brook, Summerside, Charlottetown, and Mississauga from 2008-2010.

Acknowledgements

This Youth Inquiry Project was possible because of the immediate and sustained support of Casey Brown and her belief in placing "Kids First!" In addition, this project would not have been possible without the financial support of the following sponsors:

Individual sponsors

Casey Brown, Dr. Anna Redden, Nancy MacDonald, Tom Bourque, Rod Hyde, Dayle Hyde, John Ryan, anonymous donors

Corporate sponsors

Heritage Memorials, Air Canada, Dexter Construction, Imperial Oil, Oilsands Discovery Centre, Total

Educational sponsors

Prime Minister's Award for Excellence in Teaching, Fort McKay School, Avon View High School, Hants West Local of the Nova Scotia Teachers Union, RCH (Race Relations, Cross Cultural Understanding, and Human Rights) of the Annapolis Valley Regional School Board

Community sponsors

Fort McKay IRC, Fort McKay Daycare, Fort McKay Wellness Centre

Gifts provided by

CNRL, Syncrude, Suncor, Shell, Total, Imperial Oil, Fort McKay Wellness Centre, Fort McKay Group of Companies, Fort McKay First Nation, Fort McKay School

Contents organized by inquiry questions

Contents organized by essay structure

1

Defining a community

Garrett Nelson

"For a community to be whole and healthy, it must be based on people's love and concern for each other."[1]
- Millard Fuller, Founder of Habitat for Humanity

How many ways can you define the term "community"? The definition of the term "community" is constantly evolving as modern-day communities continue to change. I have interviewed many of my peers, some who know each other and many who do not. Some live in the same communities and some live on the other side of the world. Most were peers my own age in high school or university and their experiences with local communities would be expected to be different from the experiences of people on the other side of the world. Surprisingly enough, when asked, "How would you define the term 'community'?" the responses could be summed up into five broad categories.

---

1 I have used a quote as a method of catching the reader's attention. It is straight-forward and the reader now knows the point of my essay, if they could not grasp it from the title.

In order to define a community, we should consider the types of communities that exist. I decided that there are two main types of communities: a physical community (which means that the people live in the same areas) and an online community (which means that the people do not necessarily live near each other, but instead communicate via the internet). I have received input from my friends in physical communities as well as online communities and it can be said that the two are relatively the same in how they are defined. Keeping in mind the different opinions which I have accumulated from many sources, below I offer five definitions of the term "community."

1. *A community is a group of people who share a common interest, or an aspect of their lives.* This type of community is not limited to the physical area in which people live, as there are many ways to share an interest with people without living near them since the advent of the internet. Common interests in a physical community could be the expansion of the community and the well-being of the community members, where the interests of an online community could be finding a place to chat, or talking about things that the whole community enjoys.[2]

2. *A community is a group of people, regardless of where they live, who are willing to help each other.* In a community, there is a sense of belonging and the people are unified by one means or another. This is another case where the internet can create a community, such as an online support group. In a physical community, there is an implied sense of belonging in the community after living with the other members for a long time.

3. *A community is a common area for people who are a part of a social group and are willing to work together towards a certain goal.* This type of community is usually a physical community,

---

2 By using a direct example of some things which would fit into this definition, I am giving the reader a better idea of what a community is, which will help them further understand the overall idea.

but an online community is also able to be social and to work together. A common area is not necessarily a physical room in which people talk, but can be understood to be a place where people can gather and talk, such as an online chat room, or a community center.[3]

4. *A community is an interworking network of people and/or objects that have a direct connection to each other through technology or not.* This group can exist regardless of their purposes or goals. This type of community is more likely to be an online community since the premise of most online communities is to allow members to interact with each other through a network. That being said, a physical community could belong in this definition, since people are capable of becoming a physical network through which information can be exchanged to other members of the community, not just through technology, but through word of mouth.

5. *A community is a place in which there is encouraged communication.* This communication happens on a regular basis. In order to have a thriving community, there must be active communication by the people of the community, be it in person, over Facebook, MSN, or by posting on an online forum.[4] A community will only succeed if the members are willing to communicate with each other. This is possible in both physical and online communities. In personal experience, an online community relies on communication more than a physical community does, simply because a physical community has other ways of keeping the community together, such as living together.

---

[3] By saying what a community is not, I am using a technique called "negation." This technique puts the concept into a better context by explaining what it is *not*. In this situation, readers can understand what I mean by the term "common room" because I have explained what it is *not*.

[4] By putting the definition in context, the definition essay becomes more practical to the reader and allows them to relate to what is being defined.

Defining community as "a place where people live together" is enough for most people. However, a community is not simply "a place where people live together."[5] The complexity of defining a community has been a major challenge for many years. In 1955, a book was published identifying 94 different definitions of the term "community." While this is a large number of definitions, during my survey of friends, family, acquaintances, and peers from as far away as Australia, I received definitions and examples which could be simplified into five different categories. I think this is why it is important to define the term "community" over and over as time goes on, because the idea of a community is constantly evolving. As our world becomes more and more connected, our ideas are constantly changing due to the opinions of other people. Our ideas are constantly being influenced by others, and having a reference point for how communities exist is something that could benefit us all.

[5] This is another example of negation. When used in a conclusion, it helps to remind the reader of what they just learned, and reinforce the earlier points of the essay.

2

Passing it down: The importance of culture
Stephen Long

With the label of their given name, communities may often be misrepresented, as these given names do very little to elaborate on the characteristics specific to that community. Each community across Canada—and the world for that matter—has cultural characteristics that are particular to the area as well as other characteristics that they share with various communities. Through the study of what is deemed important and necessary to pass on to the younger generations, we can learn what a community values and which aspects of their culture a community would like to see continued.

The study of culture in Hants County, Nova Scotia can allow one to identify several definite cultural characteristics which are passed on to the children in the area. One of these aspects of our culture is the need to become successful in our careers; accumulating wealth, demanding respect from others in our profession, and achieving our personal best in that which we pursue. In our community, the inability to acquire these attributes may oftentimes lead those who have gained the social status of "successful" to frown upon those who haven't been so fortunate. This negative view that many have is another reason for some to strive for the success that most parents desire for their children. From my perspective, this wealth-orientated definition of success is one example of what the people of Hants County wish for their children.[6]

Fort McKay is a small First Nations community of 500 to 600 people located roughly an hour north of Fort McMurray, Alberta. During our exploration of the area, I noticed many things that are similar to that which I am used to in Nova Scotia; the landscape was quite alike in some ways, the amount of snow was not new to me, and many of the trees were similar to those of Hants County. The people however were another story. In Fort McKay the outdoors was as much a home as the structures which had been built. Over hundreds of years, the people of the area developed many techniques and strategies, as well as customs and beliefs pertaining to "the bush." Trapping, logging, and cabin-building each have their own set order of skills and tradition to be followed which are generally passed down from parent to child, allowing the traditions to be continued.[7]

While in Hants County our parents wish us to acquire wealth in the form of currency and have a large monetary value, in Fort McKay a different type of wealth is desired for the younger generation. While a monetary wealth is not deemed unnecessary, a wealth of knowledge pertaining to the land and its importance is also stressed to the children.[8]

Oftentimes that which the parent desires for their children is not attained. Oftentimes the goal or expectation of the parent conflicts with the child's will and own desires. The sweet temptation of a chocolate bar or the tingle of a ketchup chip just before you bite into it can often be much more persuasive than the nagging voice of a parent or guardian demanding that you look after your health.

---

6 Here I used one paragraph entirely devoted to Hants County and the common characteristics of Hants County communities.

7 Immediately following the paragraph on Hants County, I wrote about a similar characteristic of Fort McKay in order to allow these communities to be easily compared.

8 After a paragraph devoted to each community, I used another paragraph to link the two together and make my own comparisons of the communities.

Complaints of obesity and general lack of bodily well being are often heard across Hants County, yet for some reason much of the younger generation are unable to maintain a healthy lifestyle, despite the relentless nagging of their parents as well as many others in their day-to-day life. This is an example of the general consensus among the people of Hants County, and what they would like to see for their children.

Another aspect of culture deemed important to be passed on to the younger generation in Fort McKay is the need for an education. Every community member we spoke to in Fort McKay who was over the age of twenty understood the value education and the major role in plays in the lives of all people today. However, in Fort McKay it is not simply math and science taught in the classrooms. The education system has been developed to allow the traditions and culture to be passed down to the children. Some classes require the students to create and present a traditional dress of their people, while other classes teach traditional dancing. In addition, the languages of Cree and Dene are taught in some classrooms. The educators in Fort McKay do an excellent job of incorporating the traditions and culture of their people into the school environment. While the importance of being fit and healthy is not forgotten in Fort McKay, the importance of incorporating culture into their education is a high priority to the people of Fort McKay.

While studying the concept of communities in Fort McKay, I realized that while many people would like to see culture and tradition passed down to the younger generations there are more important issues to be addressed. Some communities have faced terrible hardships in their past and Fort McKay is one of them. In the 1950s a residential school was set up for all children between the ages of five and fifteen. In these residential schools, many of the students were forced to undergo hardships many of us will never know. Forbidden to use their own language, and stripped of all love and compassion, many of the children grew up without parental figures. Once they were released from the residential schools, people returned to their communities and started their own families without being properly prepared to care for their children. Thus, those children who attended residential schools grew up without being exposed to proper parenting. According to some, a cycle of poor parenting was created and from that cycle many other problems spawned including drug and alcohol abuse, and in many cases a failure to show compassion to other forms of life. Some community members are learning how to break this cycle and are improving their quality of life.

Through my study of communities I learned what aspects of their culture the people Fort McKay and Hants County would like to see passed on to their children and therefore what it is these communities value. It is my hope that these findings will enable readers to learn about the importance of culture in their communities and become inspired to look into their own communities as to what is passed on to younger generations. Whether it is health, etiquette, traditional dancing, or the need for education, all communities have certain cultural characteristics they pass down; it is the variation in the characteristics which sets them apart as a unique community.[9]

[9] For my conclusion, I bring the main ideas together and remind the reader of the kind of thinking I was hoping to inspire, while attempting to leave room for the reader's own thoughts on the subject.

3

Cultural traditions in the 21st century

Barrett Mason

Growing up in a rural community, my parents have always had a strong belief in having religion in my upbringing. I attended church throughout my childhood and received the sacraments. However, I was one of very few regular church attendees in their youth, as the majority of the congregation sported grey and white hair. I was the only person to receive my sacrament of confirmation in my church of over fifty regular attendees. The fact of the matter is religion is no longer as important to everyday life in my community as it was in former generations.

For that matter, many traditions that were once a major part of former generations are less important to the youth of today.[10] In years past, many families in my community owned and operated farms, trades, and other enterprises that were traditionally passed down from generation—the so-called "family business." However, nowadays most young people will leave the family in search of their own path, seeking independence from the rest of the family.[11]

[10] In a cause and effect essay, the thesis focuses on the particular trend or phenomena being described.

[11] Each paragraph presents a separate thought containing a cause, effect, or both.

One reason for the changes can be attributed to the changing family unit. Many youth in my community have two full-time employed parents who have less time to spend with their children. It is no longer the norm for grandparents to move in with their children and grandchildren in older age, as they often instead inhabit senior housing complexes. Due to the lack of time spent together, youth will often be less concerned or interested in learning traditions pertaining to their personal culture.[12]

To live in the twenty-first century means to be more connected with the rest of the world than ever before. We have become dependent on our televisions, cell phones, MP3 players, and perhaps the godfather of information—the internet. Armed with these tools, youth are able to gain their own avenue to their peers, popular culture, and to mass information that would have been unimaginable even thirty years ago. With the ability to gain access to these things, youth gain a feeling of independence that separates us from dependence on our guardians. This connection between youth and their elders is critical in the continuation of traditional culture, and without it, many traditions are fated to end.

Yet does this mean that all traditional culture will become a thing of the past? Twenty-first century technology also has advantages to our cultural advancement.[13] The sharing of information has opened doors to massive amounts of cultural data becoming available. Light can be shed on little-known civilizations, and formerly intricate and difficult practices can be explained in detail and made available to almost anyone. Audio recording devices can be used to preserve oral traditions that have been passed down for generations. The creation of these devices has allowed our cultures to be spread and introduced to others.

---

[12] Referring back to the thesis statement of the essay creates clearer links to the thoughts being explained and the central purpose of the text.

[13] Discussing alternate effects of a certain cause helps to build more sympathy for both sides of the argument. This can also be a means of anticipating a reader's counter-claim.

Fort McKay, Alberta is an example of a transitioning culture.[14] The First Nations people have inhabited the area for thousands of years. Named in 1912 by the Hudson's Bay Company, the land has a rich history of Aboriginal traditions such trapping, moccasin making, and traditional medicine. These practices were passed down from generation to generation, defining the culture. However, this is quickly changing. With changing times and economy, many fur trappers were forced to abandon their lifestyle because it could no longer sustain the cost of living. Tommy, one of a dwindling number of trappers in the area, explains: "If I had my way, I wouldn't be trapping. But, I want to keep this…it's part of my heritage."

The First Nations community of Fort McKay is undergoing changes and many people are searching for their cultural identity. Some still maintain traditions, yet others want nothing to do with traditions. Large oil companies exploiting the surrounding land provide a way of life for many residents there, offering an alternative, more sustainable way of life than traditional lifestyles. In order to survive, the people must be willing to adapt to their changing surroundings. This may cause the loss of traditions.[15]

Twenty-first century technology connects us to a much larger community than what exists within our immediate neighbourhood. Many different cultures are succumbing and assimilating to the popular culture of our time. More foreign cultures are undergoing a process of cultural globalization which is dominated by the trend of *Westernization.* Westernization is a means in which, through media outlets, the culture adapts to mirror that of the popular culture of the Western World.[16]

---

[14] I used a real-world case of causes and the effect on a community. The example helps the reader understand how the cause and effect may (or will) play out in real life.

[15] Using real-world examples in the conclusion helps prepare readers for the closing arguments.

[16] Here, I make a series of connections, moving from smaller, more specific cases of the cause and effect to a much larger, global scale.

The growths of free trade and economic globalization have had a direct impact on cultures worldwide. Western franchises are expanding into foreign markets, and are being absorbed by the surrounding culture. "Think about a Starbucks in the middle of the Forbidden City - Beijing China. This is a reality!" says Seamus Marriot, former vice principal of Shanghai American School and current Principal of Cairo American College.[17] "The shrinking of our world in the global context has made everything more accessible. Global media and the expansion of corporate ventures or the global economy have influenced society and culture around the world."

Music is another area where Western society is influencing the youth. "Yes there are popular Arabic singers, but they are greatly over shadowed by the 'big stars' from the West. Shakira performing in front of the Pyramids of Giza was an absolute 'must-have-a-ticket' event for many young Egyptians," said Mr. Marriot. "Not exactly what the Pharaoh had in mind for his burial place!"

In a lot of ways, the advances in technology and communication have allowed us to become more familiar with different cultures and practices worldwide. Better understanding and documentation has created a web of knowledge that would have been unimaginable prior to these times.[18] However, the twenty-first century is altering many aspects of traditional culture for the next generation. Losing these traditions would be losing a large part of what separates us human beings from each other and makes us culturally unique. Customs define cultures, and without culture, we lose our identities.[19]

---

[17] A first-hand quote creates a more personal tone for the reader and brings the writing "to life." I obtained this quote through personal email correspondence.

[18] Two perspectives in the conclusion allow a less biased essay and leave the reader more open to a wider range of opinions.

[19] The conclusion recaps the key points of the cause and effect, and also relates the effect to the reader in how it can impact people.

Local industry: The community member with a life of its own

Blake Smith

The local industry of a community is really just like any member of the community.[20] Industry easily becomes a core part of the community once it takes root. In fact, industry can quickly become dependant on its community to keep growing and thriving. The two quickly develop a fascinating type of relationship that after enough time can become very hard to part with. Any local industry brings many challenges along with many benefits for any community. To some, a community is defined by its people, but it can also be said that people come to define themselves by the industry in their community.

Industry is really born when it is placed into a stable community.[21] Communities of any size cannot truly survive without some type of

---

20 Picking the specific topic is the first step in any explanation/informative essay. The topic I chose to address was how local industry grows. I use personification to help readers connect with this idea.

21 It made sense for this essay to start with industry being born. As an explanatory/informative essay, this analogy was the best way I could allow the topic to unfold.

industry. People living in communities with a stable industry want to stay. The community and industry combined bring each other what they need. People flock to the community as the industry begins to grow and the community provides a place for the industry to expand and attract supportive businesses.[22] After an industry has been around a while, it begins to grow and starts to give back to its community. Unlike a person, when an industry grows the rest of the community grows along with it both in terms of its population and its economic growth. A mall, for instance, is more inclined to be established in a community that has a growing industry and an upward population trend. It would be more of a risk for any business, such as a mall, to come into a community that does not have a stable industry.

This seems to be the very problem that my community is facing; we have no major industry that attracts people to the area. We really don't have much of a mall and I don't see that changing anytime soon. There is not a whole lot going on in terms of economic development. This is quite a contrast to how the town was in the late 90s: the opening of the street called Cole Drive was seen as a big boost to the town's economy. The big editions to the town were a McDonalds, a Tim Horton's, and then in 2000, an Atlantic Super Store. It seemed like the town was going through a real economic boom. But sadly, nothing substantial has really come of it. Our town has remained relatively stagnate in its growth.

As with anything that is growing, industry is bound to run into some rough spots as it goes along its path of expansion.[23] There will always be critics: some who think that industry oversteps it boundaries in the name of self-growth. A common and controversial boundary for an industry is the industry's relationship to the

---

[22] This idea came to me when I observed that many of the business in Fort McMurray would not be there without the oilsands.

[23] I chose to introduce a new stage in the industry's life with topic sentences to help with the flow of the essay. It makes sense to have the rebellious stage of the industry come after there has been some early growth. The analogy is useful in presenting the ideas in a sequence that is easy to follow.

local environment.[24] This seems to be a roadblock for many industries. It is easy to make comparisons between a business at this stage of growth and an adolescent: both are not really sure of their capabilities. Both want to try their best but there are many obstacles in the way and at times, there can be a serious lack of support. That's how a growing business must feel when it tries to expand and is met with resistance. On the other hand, the residents of the community may be unsure of the industry's intentions. This seems to be the case in Fort McKay where residents are aware of the positives effects that the oilsands industry brings to the area, yet there are also the ever-looming negative effects on the environment in the community.

Industries have to learn to mature along with the rest of the members of the community. The local industry is able to do a lot of good for its community. Like any community member, the industry might be looking for a way to prove to its peers that it can help the local community grow and become better. Like any person, the local industry is a powerful tool that can be used to bring the community together. In order to keep local industries alive they may at times require the help of all the members of their community. They might need to remind the community of what they have done for them over the years, or spread awareness about upcoming events that can bring new life to the community. The oilsands project in Fort McKay is nowhere near the end of its existence; the growth that it has to achieve is almost as vast as the deposits of oil themselves.

There is no doubt that industry greatly defines a community. A lot of the time big or any size industry can develop a poor reputation, but in reality, they do more than they are given credit. They give people the comfort that they can come home every night and know that when they wake up the next day they will still have a job to go to and a way to provide for themselves and their family. It would be a scary to live in a world where industries do not partner

[24] I thought of this idea when visiting Fort McKay and learned how this community has had to deal with this issue because of the oilsand industry's environmental impact on the community.

with communities to become part of the community's identify. Local industry is a much as a member of any community as you and I. Industry may contribute to the community in a different way and is met with a lot of criticism and uncertainty, but is that really any different than another newcomer to a community? The only way an industry can really grow and survive in a community is if the members of the community are there to support the industry. The local industry is really as much a part of any community as the people that are in it. It is born, lives, grows, and comes to an end with its community.[25]

[25] One of the most important parts of an explanation/informative essay is to keep the language simple so that readers can follow it easily. I tried throughout the essay to keep things simple.

5

After high school: The effects of industry on attitudes towards post-secondary studies

Mairi MacEachern

The same question runs through every high school student's mind: "What am I going to do after graduation?" The answers of course vary from student to student but did you know that they also very from town to town? Depending on where you are, and what industries surround you, your knowledge of what opportunities exist is limited.[26] For instance, did you know that working at a pulp mill you could make on average fifty thousand dollars a year before benefits? Or that a farmer could make over eighty thousand dollars annually? Or that without graduating from high school you can make sixty-five thousand dollars a year? I wouldn't have known this from my everyday experiences in my community because jobs like these don't surround my everyday life. As humans we learn more by what we see than what we hear, and since where we live directly relates to what we can see, we tend to have biased opinions as to which industry is most important to us and what level of education is most important to our society as a whole.

---

[26] Even though entertainment isn't the point of an explanation essay, you still need something at the beginning to grab the reader's attention. Here, I use questions and bold statements to engage the reader.

Industries are what define how our town, country, and world function. No matter what career choice you pick you will become part of an industry. According to www.dictionary.com an industry is "any general business activity."[27] We need all industries in order to maintain the lifestyle that we have become accustomed to within our society. For instance, without the oil industry, we wouldn't be able to use cars, buses, or planes as our main forms of transportation. A lot of people would also have to change the way that they heat their homes because oil would no longer be an option. The loss of the oil and gas industry would also take its toll on other industries such as the pulp and paper industry. People might change their main form of heat from oil to wood, therefore using more wood than we already consume. Without each industry, our world as we know it would deteriorate.

When most people hear the word "industry" the first thing they think about is a big factory utilizing our natural resources. However, industries are more than that. Yes, the steel, oil, and paper industries have large factories but what about the tourism industry? Or the agricultural industry? Or what about an industry that you may have never have heard about before but almost everyone has considered entering—the knowledge industry. This is where I feel that my future is directed.

For the majority of my life I have grown up in a community designed for people with either university degrees or minimum wage jobs, and nothing in between. My town is full of nurses, teachers, and businesspersons—people who in short, belong to the knowledge industry. Because of this, I feel that my life has been directed towards going to work within the knowledge industry. From what I've seen in my life, if I want to make more than minimum wage I must go to university and this means directing all of my life choices onto a path that will get me there. Even the adults I have spoken with seem to think that the best way to make a living is to go to university. Earlier this year I went to speak with my guidance coun-

[27] In order for the reader to get the most out of your essay they must clearly understand what you are talking about. Having a clarifying sentence helps.

sellor about what I should do after I graduate high school, and she too handed me pamphlets from different universities and asked me to write down what seemed interesting to me and then come back later.[28] Not once did she mention being a farmer or a hairdresser or even a pipefitter (which I could get a job doing almost immediately and make approximately $75,000 annually). We need all of these occupations in order to sustain the lifestyle we are used to so why didn't she suggest any of those?

Communities tend to be very different in the ways in which they influence young people to think about life after high school. Most students in northern Alberta feel that their future will be in the oil industry. The choices they make in regards to their education are quite different from mine because of where they live. They know that they can make thirty dollars an hour without finishing high school. Or if you do graduate, you can make over $100,000 dollars a year. In choosing this industry, you don't go into huge debt and you can reap the rewards almost immediately. This is the dominant message about life after high school that surrounds students in northern Alberta; it may also be what their parents, aunts, uncles and siblings discuss within their families. Of course, there are teachers and nurses, and businesspersons in northern Alberta as well, but they don't make as much money. Because the high school students don't see these occupations as frequently, they may not immediately think of being in the knowledge industry after high school. The same is true for me: because I don't see pipefitters and heavy equipment operators everyday, the oil industry won't be my immediate consideration for options for after high school.

Education is a hassle to most people—something you must go through in order to be able to succeed in life; it is a stepping stone not the final result.[29] So, if you could skip that step, why wouldn't you? The industry we choose to pursue after high school deter-

---

[28] Adding a personal anecdote to your essay helps to keep the reader's attention as well as helps to deliver the information in a way so that it is straightforward and clear. This is important point to keep in mind when writing an explanation essay.

[29] I used a metaphor here to describe education as part of life's journey.

mines the amount of education we must acquire. If we were to choose an industry that does not value education, would we ourselves value education? On the other hand, if we choose an industry that requires and values continued education, our success might be measured by the extent in which we embrace lifelong learning.[30]

[30] This sentence required some extra thought; it was difficult to keep from making the information seem persuasive instead of explanatory.

Responding to discrimination

Becky Swinamer

My first experience with discrimination was watching a movie as a child.[31] I never experienced discrimination in school or anywhere in the community. If somebody hated somebody else it was due to something that person did and not for any other reason. As I got older and into high school, I realized that not every community was the same—I lived in one community and went to school in another. My school community did not feel the same way. People were actually discriminated against in classrooms by teachers and in the hallway on break by other students. That being said, in this small town community it wasn't really an issue and was always informally addressed.

The incident happened at a local fast-food restaurant when a white employee said derogatory things about a black customer. The white employee then said them to a black employee. The black employee complained to the manager and the white employee that said the comments was fired. That was the first instant that I ever heard of anything being done about anything involving matters of discrimination.

---

[31] Starting off with my own experience helps readers relate to the subject matter.

Discrimination is treatment taken toward or against a person of a certain social group based on an assumed class or category. So whether it is race, age, or gender,[32] everyone can face discrimination. People around the world face different forms of discrimination from schooling prejudice to attacks on lifestyles and beliefs systems.

In what ways does a community respond to discrimination, be it ostracization or indifference? Communities can be very tight-knit with a strong sense of support. For example, in some communities, there are Wellness Centres[33] where children can receive care for free while the parents work fifteen-hour shifts. Resources in a community can be found locally, if you trust people in the community. If you are hurt due to discrimination you could rely on people in your community rather than internalizing the experience. It is important to note that some people within a community can be tight-knit but also face a great deal of discrimination. For example, inner-racial discrimination can take place such as when someone unfairly accuses someone else of something because one person is Cree and the other is Chippewa. According to my conversations with some community members in Fort McKay, this does happen, but is a less common form of discrimination.

When a community shows discriminatory beliefs, it's likely to be an effective indicator of the public atmosphere for minority groups in the future of the community. I believe that all visible minority communities experience the indignities and wounds of systemic discrimination whether it be the government (provincial and federal) at fault or the said community. When I spoke to the principal of a First Nation elementary school, she described how when she took her students out to a restaurant they were spit on and the waiter will not wait on them.

---

[32] Here, I expand the original question and broaden my argument.

[33] A Wellness Center is a place where children can go after-school from 3-9 pm to eat supper and play. In Fort McKay, the Wellness Centre is sponsored by industry partners.

Discrimination based on gender doesn't appear to be as significant a problem in some communities as racial discrimination. For example, women in the oilsand industry in Fort McKay have equal employment opportunities but this does not necessarily mean that they don't face gender-based discrimination on a daily basis.[34] In speaking with some of the female oilsands workers, I learned that some male workers have a hard time respecting women as their equals and say derogatory things to them.

It is important to acknowledge the possible "domino effect" where if a family is discriminatory then the child in that family is more likely to think the same way and therefore begin a cycle of discrimination. A cycle of discrimination is challenging for a community and a society. I suspect that the numbers of children that enter school with discriminatory beliefs are the same numbers that leave. This is not to say that the curriculum doesn't teach effectively; this may be due to the strong influence of parents and guardians. Instead of changing students, we should focus on changing the parents. Some schools and communities have "Family Fun Nights" and other get-together nights. These are activities that try to increase the amount of parent/guardian interaction with their kids.

I heard a story about a First Nations woman who had arthritis in her ankles and had to start using crutches. One day she lost her balance in a mall and fell down. Instead of being helped up, she was gawked at and called names and no one would help her because she was First Nations. This goes to show that even a community that is primarily First Nations still shows racism by the other races and social groups moving into the community. Community awareness is an aspect that is perhaps overlooked by some communities. Without community awareness there can be severe consequences where youth can have limited possibilities for fulfilling their potential.[35]

---

[34] Here, I am using a counter-argument to emphasize my original point.

[35] Rather than ending with a question or opinion, I use a statement to emphasize the narrative style of this essay.

7

Meeting Anna: The cycle of poverty

Stephanie Adams

Poverty is a cycle spinning out of control in society. Even closer to home, poverty is found within the geographical boundaries of our own communities. In today's twenty-first century, communities have devised unique tools in order to address poverty. As I have become more mature, a greater comprehension about my world has resulted in my quest for answers to this systemic issue which currently feeds the status quo within many communities. I struggle, questioning how, or if, communities can initiate and support a paradigm shift around the underlying causes and effects of poverty.

As the early morning sun began to peek though the broken windowpane beside Anna's[36] mattress, she slowly sat up listening to the train-whistle echoing in the distance. Its daily routine was repeated as it carried the enormous load of gypsum from the mine.

[36] Anna is a fictional character who represents various children who experience times of poverty in my community. In a narrative essay, it is important to establish the characters and their situation within the first paragraph. This helps eliminate any confusion and allows the reader to gain immediately knowledge about the characters.

Anna yawned and slid her tiny feet onto the cold floor. Shivers swept through her as she made her way to the empty kitchen. Her cat greeted her with a hiss and a cry of hunger. Anna patted the cat for a few moments before slipping into the jeans and sweater she'd worn yesterday. Stepping outside, she headed to church.

As she knelt in her pew, Anna repeated the same prayers that she had been saying for five years. She prayed for love, money and a better future, and wished she could be one of the lucky kids in West Hants. The door behind her squeaked open and one of her teachers from her school entered. Anna turned her head trying to make herself invisible. Ms.Kerr[37] knelt down beside her and explained that she had an idea that might be helpful to Anna's little sister. She wanted her to be part of the three-year old screening program. Ms.Kerr explained that the program was used by the school board to help identify children who may need more support in school at a very young age. Anna liked this idea. Besides, anything that would make Molly's experience at school more pleasant was worth a try. Ms.Kerr excused herself and returned to her seat for the remainder of the service.

At the end of mass, Anna went to the back room just like she did every Sunday. As usual, Margaret and Paul, local volunteers, greeted her with a warm hug. Anna smiled and skipped to her seat by the window. They joined her, bringing a steaming warm bowl of soup. Anna's stomach growled with hunger. The apple she swallowed on her way over hadn't been nearly enough to keep her stomach full. As she ate, Paul and Margaret chatted and told her jokes. Anna giggled as she handed them the empty bowl, and pulled out her school books. The three of them set to work looking over Anna's homework assignments and proofreading her stories. Anna loved Paul and Margaret like parents. They were always there for her and Molly when their parents were out for the night or busy at work. After having one more laugh, Anna packed up her binder and said goodbye to her favorite volunteers. They handed her a backpack filled with some well-needed groceries and

---

[37] Ms. Kerr is a fictional character who represents various teachers who support the children in their schools.

a new outfit for her and her sister. As Anna headed home, she thought about how lucky she was to have such wonderful friends like she did at church. They worked hard to make sure those in need were looked after as best as they could.

***

Monday morning was the first time I'd noticed Anna standing by the breakfast table in the foyer at our school. Her faded jeans and wrinkled shirt made me appreciate the new sweater I was wearing. I wondered whether Anna always ate at school, whether she woke up cold, whether she had anyone to talk to, and what her home life was like. Mrs.Derouche[38] brought down another steaming plate of food and Anna smiled, thanking her. Other students grabbed food from the cart. Just like Anna, they depended on programs such as the *Breakfast Program*, to provide food for them. Without it, they would be hungry and less learning would occur throughout their day as a result of not having the necessary nutrition. Instead, they had the opportunity to learn the importance of an education, and hopefully break free from the grips of poverty.

The true impact of one good deed is better appreciated when examined in a more in-depth manner. My desire to contribute to my community was first fulfilled when I had the chance to take a collegial role in planning a "wake-a-thon" in support of families in need within my community. I was able to help children like Anna, and provide a positive influence on their lives. After seeing Anna for the first time the week before, I was motivated to support something of value—something that would make a difference in her life. Volunteering in a time of need is a powerful tool in the war against poverty, and it's a tool used nationwide. Having successfully raised funds for our local Christmas charity, I could see first hand the necessity and value of helping others in my commu-

[38] Mrs.Derouche is the coordinator of the *Breakfast Program* at Avon View High School. She volunteers her time every weekday to ensure free food is available for those in need. Numerous schools in West Hants provide a similar breakfast program for their students with the help of funding from local businesses and organizations, as well as from individual donations.

nity. I realized right away that Anna would benefit from what we had accomplished.

I know Anna will have the support of many others in my community as West Hants provides multiple resources in order to address poverty. Without the support Anna needs at home, she struggles in school and avoids social interaction. I hope that when and if the time comes, Anna will choose to continue her learning at the *Hants Learning Association.*[39] Because 7500 adults in the municipality are without their grade 12 diploma, educational initiatives such as this are positive and pro-social ways of identifying and connecting with those in the community like Anna who are most at risk to becoming trapped in the cycle of poverty. With improved literacy skills, they are more prepared and qualified for opportunities such as new employment.

Having recently traveled to Fort McKay, Alberta, I had the privilege of witnessing unique tools the community uses when dealing with its poverty, and I immediately wished Anna could have such opportunities. The local school not only provided the *Breakfast Program*, but a *Fruit Exchange Program* as well, with the support of a local company, Total. Having the opportunity to trade junk food for fresh fruit gave the students healthier alternatives that weren't available at home. As a donation, the school offers the junk food to a neighbouring community's *Centre of Hope*, a place where homeless people can go for shelter.[40] Casey Brown, the school's current principal in Fort McKay, strives to make the lives of the children and people around her better. To her, donating one-hundred and fifty dollars worth of socks to the *Centre of Hope* is an easy, yet meaningful task. She works hard to give the children opportunities they wouldn't have without outside help. A program in place at school such as the *Book Bonus*, where one child receives a book each school day, is only one tool that she uses to advocate for her students' well-being. *The Mothers of Fort McKay* program at the new

---

[39] The Hants Learning Association was formed as a result of strong volunteers such as the late Patricia Helliwell.

[40] Limiting the amount of detail is important when writing a narrative essay. Too much detail can distract the reader from the main focus of the piece.

daycare centre offers free assistance to mothers in need. *Meals on Wheels* helps elders with their nutritional needs, and the *Community Development Team* evaluates the programs and ensures new programs are introduced to the community as needed. In situations where poverty leads to any number of challenges, community members showed me the power in combining dedication and creative programs when funding is readily available. It makes me ponder whether Anna would gain more confidence if she had programs available to her such as these.[41]

As a privileged youth in a twenty-first century community, I feel that positive progress can be made in each community and I feel compelled to contribute. The answer to the systemic cycle of poverty is not going to be found by limiting our attention to within our own unique communities or relying on short-term assistance. A collective analysis of tools and education utilized in other communities allows us to re-evaluate the strategies used against poverty within our own municipality. Such reflection and willingness to adapt will help our communities interrupt the vicious cycle of poverty that is such a barrier to success in the lives of people like Anna.

---

[41] Following a chronological order allows the reader to follow the main point of the essay. Anna's situation was introduced early, and followed by examples of tools from within her community. Continuing with examples from communities outside the area expanded the possible options available to help people like Anna. Finally, a reflection at the end allowed the reader to make final conclusions.

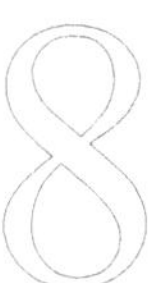

Women and 21st century communities
Samantha Harding

What does it mean to be a woman in a 21st century community?[42] I cannot tell you directly through personal experience, for a community is not something significant to me. I have no community in the sense of a neighborhood, or a stable group of people that surrounds and includes me. Although I do not have this immediate connection to others, technology makes it accessible. It can take our relationships and awareness a step further. This growing technology has allowed me to empathize and understand women from all around the world. I am now able to see how diverse women are, and how drastically their rights vary. Women's connections to their community can depend on their location, lifestyle, beliefs, and circumstances. Once analyzing the many variations of how women relate to their communities, I have identified an issue that is not often considered. This issue surrounds the women who have many rights, yet they adapt to men's expectations and the media's manipulation. Women in 21st century communities must continue their pursuit for equality.

[42] Starting the essay with a question allows the reader to assess what the concept means to them.

Women have various roles in their communities that depend on several factors. Where women reside, how they were brought up, and their current living situation will easily influence their position within a community. There are women with lives forced to revolve around motherhood, homecare and maintaining their husband's happiness. In these communities, they are assigned only one role, and if they were to neglect or avoid these expectations, they could face serious consequence. There are also women on the other end of the spectrum, who will go through years of education to obtain high social status and a top-paying job. Many of these women put their family life and relationships on hold to further themselves in their career. Women that are too focused on their profession may end up missing out on the chance to have a family.[43] I think that a balance is in order, where every woman has the chance to make a choice that is completely her own. It's okay for a woman to embrace a family life without having a steady career and it is okay for a woman to concentrate solely on her work. The problem presents itself when women feel pressure from their community and the influential people in their lives. Women's roles in their community greatly depend on beliefs and expectations.

Women have very diverse situations and rights. We have yet to obtain uniform equality. Our communities differ so greatly that defining a woman in the 21st century could never be narrowed down to a particular group or statement. There are women still trapped within strict and negative circumstance. Their rights to an education, a job, the choice in having children, as well as the choice in who they marry, whether they marry, and what age they marry is taken away from them. I wish I could passionately state that all women in 21st century communities experience complete equality and status. I anticipate the day that we live in a world where each and every woman feels adequate. This question of what it means to be a woman in a 21st century community could mean anything from a woman that is able to run her own life and make her own decisions, to a woman that was snatched from her childhood,

[43] By comparing two very different situations, I can demonstrate to the readers how women's rights are not in unison, and that their roles vary depending on circumstances and expectations.

starved of rights, and forced to comply with men. Women are focused on the future and equality, but many still have rights that are comparable to the past.

Women are benefiting from advancements in their rights, but they still succumb to powerful influence. This is an issue that demands our focus. Women are shaping themselves to suit men, the media, and society at large. Women are undergoing plastic surgery, covering-up with makeup, drastically altering their hair, and always searching for the next beauty miracle. I have become accustomed to this lifestyle, and it sickens me that I am physically unable to leave my house without the mask I apply every morning. I have to portray an image that can meet society's beauty standards.[44] I, like many other women, would never go out into the world as my natural self. I prefer this being I've created from bought goods, what the media has shown me, and how this look appeals to society and to men. Many women are consumed with their image, altering themselves to suit others' needs and desires. Appearance is not the only factor affected, for women also disguise their personality to appeal to others. I have strong opinions concerning women's rights,[45] but like many others, I still struggle to portray what society thinks a woman in this century should be.

There is not a single definition to describe what it means to be a woman in a 21st century community, for we are living in an extremely diverse era. Every woman has a different role and relationship with the concept. Many women are struggling with rights, even within their communities. They have to fight for equality, or settle with uncontrollable circumstance. I want to rethink what I am doing in my daily life, and I challenge everyone to do the same. I have many rights previously earned for me, yet I still feel

---

[44] By adding in my personal conflict with society's influence, I present myself on the same human level as the reader. It shows my personal concern for the issue.

[45] By explaining that I have strong opinions for women's rights, I better explain the issue at hand. This highlights the power of manipulation and that even women passionate about women's rights may give way to dominant trends and social influences.

that I must look beautiful and strive for perfection in order to be socially accepted. I challenge us not to only be concerned for people without rights, but to evaluate the way women present themselves in a male-dominated society. Women should not be easily influenced by what the media portrays as womanly, or feel the need to change just to grasp the attention of a man. I state this concern not in a negative way, but as a challenge to all women.[46] This challenge is to be comfortable with who you are and confident in your rights. Once women start respecting themselves, everyone around them will follow their example. In 21st century communities, women need to value themselves, be valued by others, and insist upon equal opportunities.

[46] By presenting a challenge in my conclusion it gives the reader a chance to reassess what they believe a woman in a 21st century community is. It challenges us to be concerned for women in every situation, while promoting respect.

9

Media influences on communities

Duncan Armour

When talking about influencing communities there's only one spot to start with and that is the human brain.[47] The mind is easily influenced by everything around it. This is true from when we are first born and our brains are still developing, all through life until we die. We are influenced by the things we see and hear every day; the things we read, the things we watch, and even the little things we never thought mattered.

Since children minds are the most easily influenced, media often directs its attention to children. In a community like Fort McKay that is surrounded by the influence of the oil industry you would think that the kids' minds would be "hooked" on oil. It is easy to make this conclusion because the companies give communities money and it could be argued that the children must be "brought over" to value the companies in their communities. This is not necessarily the case. In my experience in Fort McKay, I learned that the largest contributing factor to the children's perception of

[47] This is an easy way to show that the essay has structure. It shows that there are a number of things that I want to point out about the topic.

society is their teachers. However, that doesn't mean modern media is out of the picture completely.

When our class was at a hockey game in Fort McMurray we watched the home team play. Here, the oil companies put a positive face to themselves. The name of the team was the "Oil Barrens."[48] This may not seem like a big deal but remember all it takes is a little push. When a child (with the most easily influenced mind) watches their home team play, they cheer their heart out not for the oil companies but for their heroes. When they think of those great moments in the hockey rink, they'll associate it with the oil companies.

I know that children are easily influenced by modern media so I wondered if the other end of the age spectrum would be completely different. As it turned out, from my perspective, the elders are not influenced at all by media. They can see straight through the media tricks. Restore the old and down with the new, right?[49] When talking with the elders from Fort McKay we learned that they may not know how to send a text message but they do know what's right for their community. One thing we heard from all of the elders is that they want the people of the community to learn. They want them to go to school, to university, and to get a job. It was great to see that the elders were still doing their duty: promoting what is best for their community. Media isn't always about modern technologies. Elders know what is influencing them and they know if the influence is good. However, some may disagree with the elders' points of view and this can create conflicts within a community when trying to determine what is right and wrong. Right and wrong can be easily tipped.

---

48 Specific examples are necessary in an expository essay such as this to strongly express your opinion. It's a way to take the big picture and narrow it down into a clear view.

49 I ask questions to see if I can get the reader to start questioning on his/her own. I begin with one point of view and then show that there are different ways of thinking. This gets the reader to think of his/her own opinion and not rely exclusively on the writer to formulate a point of view.

Think of media like an epidemic: one person is infected (1 infection) and then spreads this infection with someone else (2 infections). Then, each of them spread it to another (4 infections) and so on (8, 16, 32 infections). This metaphor is a clear example of how influential media can be. By relating media to a topic that is negatively viewed (infections), it gives you a negative view towards media.[50] Had I used an example such as family (e.g., how a family grows larger and larger each generation, adding more and more members to it) then you would have a more positive view towards media.

When you think of a town you have not been to, how can you judge it in any other way than what you've heard about it? What about a province you haven't been to? What about a country? When someone is uneducated about something, they rely on media to fill-in the blanks. Therefore media can have a "butterfly effect" on a community: the tiniest message can cause the largest understanding (or misunderstanding) of a community. Media will heavily influence the way a community examines its values, grows, and creates an identity.

---

[50] This is a way that I tried to make the reader consider what they are reading: I used a metaphor to influence the reader. With any luck they'll pause and think about what they just read and how the choice of metaphor influences perception.

10

Unreliable media
Patrick Lynch

Media shapes our perspectives of unfamiliar communities.[51] "The H1N1 flu vaccination injects a disease into your arm. Healthy people are not vulnerable to dying from the new 2009 H1N1 virus. Pregnant women should not get the 2009 H1N1 flu vaccine." A friend of mine even talked about how the vaccination was the government's plot to turn me into a zombie! Ever heard the saying, "don't trust everything you hear"? These were all false accusations that media have exploited in the past year.[52] Media such as this can aide or oppose your outlook of other cultures, communities, and races.[53]

---

51 This is a persuasive essay and is meant to persuade the reader towards something they may not originally believe.

52 www.flu.gov/news/blogs/falsemedia.html

53 Persuasive essays can have a simple form with an introductory paragraph, "body" paragraphs, and a conclusion.

Communities regularly represent themselves via the Internet.[54] The Internet—in all of its greatness—has a powerful message that people seem to think is true (you probably heard it from the Internet): the Internet is entirely free of bias. I am afraid to say it but *the internet can be biased* and it is important to know who is writing the information on the Internet. Community websites are particularly interesting to consider bias because of the information that they distribute to the reader/viewer and therefore how the community is perceived in the reader's mind. My hometown, for example, is a lovely community, with an active spirit, openness, an increasing history, and with lots of greenery and sunny days—all we're missing is *you*! This was the impression that I felt after reading my hometown website and after reading a few paragraphs, I wanted to go live in this place! Then reality started to set in and I remembered that I live in this place, although they forgot to mention that a large percentage of the community lives in retirement homes, and it is unfortunately very hard to get into the social loops of our community. Yet, if I didn't know better after looking at the website it sounded like a pretty perfect small community. I am not saying that I live in a bad community—actually quite the contrary…I really enjoy living here—it's just not what media has depicted and imposed onto us.

News is news is news, right? If this were true then we could confidently say that Al Jezeera—a Middle Eastern news broadcasting company comparable to our major Western news broadcasting companies—will have the same points of view as our local news broadcasts. With such contrasting media environments, how could it be possible for these news-broadcasting stations to have the same view? Now does news all start to seem a little too biased? Fortunately, this can be favorable; different views can open up our minds and reveal additional information, turning our worldview on its head. I think that media's job is not to change or inhibit one's mental exploration, but to open up our views of unfamiliar com-

[54] Every paragraph in the body of the essay has a beginning statement that you build on. For example, "Communities regularly represent themselves via the Internet" is my topic sentence that I use to signal the idea that I will develop in this paragraph.

munities. News isn't something that should boss you around. Instead, it should make you think, interpret, and realize that maybe the H1N1 vaccinations won't lead to a zombie apocalypse![55]

Has this happened to you: you're talking to a friend when suddenly out of the blues of their jeans a cell phone pops up and they start to text? The nerve! Their online community is more important than you? Is it your spiel on general relativity[56] that is boring your friend? Would they rather ignore the present and talk about what happened yesterday or what you might end up doing tomorrow? Well then, I guess you'll take your conversation elsewhere! The interaction between people talking to each other is what I believe to be one of the most defining characteristics of a community. How people talk to each other, what people talk about, and social behaviour is important in knowing a community. How could I go onto the Internet and figure out social interactions? It doesn't matter how beautiful a place looks or how rich a community is. If people in a community are unhappy, the community is an unhappy place. I have learned that for the most part, media such as the Internet, television, and radio, often do not or cannot describe the interactions among people in a community.

During our Youth Inquiry Project to Fort McKay, Alberta, I started to realize just how important predisposition towards a community can be. I found myself being quite biased in some of my pre-conceived opinions that were based on barrels of second-hand information I had received from media. I thought that the people of Fort McKay were helpless and before I could hear otherwise there was even a point when I believed that women's rights

---

55 When I was writing the opening paragraph, I purposely put background information about people thinking that H1N1 can turn you into a zombie, because I needed to use that information so that you can understand this little bit of comedic relief.

56 When writing a piece that is going to be displayed in society, you always have to be thinking of making the piece of text personal since that writing will have your name on it! So here I put down something that I do enjoy talking about, and although I don't know much about general relativity, I do enjoy talking about the nearly sci-fi like theories it poses and in this way I can "put my signature" on a piece of writing.

were not equal to men's rights in Fort McKay. I was wrong. The people of McKay have fought for their land rights against the oil companies and equality for women is not a predominant issue. Those three crude opinions made it difficult to think without being biased; did those perceptions that were informed by the media become internalized? It's hard enough to find the truth in media. Now I can't even trust myself to be thinking truthfully because predisposed information has tainted my knowledge. How do we know what we know about unfamiliar communities? Media is how we know, but for a person to "know" something it doesn't have to be true.[57]

I learned from the media that 500 ducks died from an accident in the oilsands. However, through a reliable contact I have found that the number was much more than media had originally suggested.[58] Media can mislead, endanger, and shape our perspectives of what lies in the unknown. Or, media can inform us, protect us, and comfort us about what lies in the future. We shouldn't leave it up to the C.E.O's of "A.B.C Corporation" or the executor of "1.2.3 Inc." to control what we know about each other. We need to take responsibility to protect what's ours—our thoughts. Escapism is nice in day-to-day stressful life but keep the fiction in the books and reality in the open, before it's too late and the fiction becomes fact.

Live in the present, dream of the past, and think about the future.

---

57 When I write my rough copy I put in a lot of "**mostly**" useless words like "just," "most," or "so." These words may sound good in your head, but when you revise your writing piece you will find "**out**" that they "**just**" get in the way of the information. They are words with no meaning and "**I find that**" when you exclude these words from your writing, the sentences flow better (e.g., all the words in bold can be removed from the text without disrupting the flow of ideas). TIP: Try keeping a personal taboo list of overused "useless words" for editing your own writing.

58 The best writing I have done is always when I am enjoying writing. Here, I had to put this little fact of the ducks in somewhere since I felt like if I excluded then it would have been painful for me. This was one of those gut-feelings that I get and this time I decided to "fly" with it.

11

Technology tidal wave

Chelsea Cox

We are considered to be in the age of technology. Thousands of different gadgets are developed each year to entertain us, assist us, and help us communicate. These gadgets can be something as small as an iPod, which is used to listen to music, or something as crucial as a direct neural interface, which is a machine that rewires frayed sensors in the brain. Technology has allowed our human race to do things that fifty years ago would have been considered impossible—but at what cost? Technology is a wonderful thing, but has it come to a point where we have become so immersed in a technology tidal wave that we are not seeing the negative repercussions that follow? Or is the digital world the future world and we must accept how the human race is evolving?

The number of times that I've walked down the street and seen young children and adults alike with a cell phone is impossible to count. Technology is slowly becoming the way people—especially the younger generations—communicate and many believe that this is an issue. People think it's an issue because the younger generations are slowly losing their interpersonal skills because texting has taken place of calling and video games have taken place of going outside and playing. The children that I see everyday are growing up in a whole different world than me, and I'm only seventeen. Children that I'm surrounded by are now content with sitting in their rooms playing the new Mario game for hours on end. With new technology children are beginning to lose the knowledge of how to interact face-to-face with a person and replace that knowledge with how to interact computer-to-computer. Interpersonal skills are so important to have. When having a conversation with someone you can gauge emotion and listen actively to make the person feel like what they are saying is important. Without these skills people are unsure of how to interact with one another and that's a huge problem. With the loss of these interpersonal skills, kids growing up do not really understand how to communicate directly with people.

However, with that being said,[59] seventy-five years ago who would have thought it would be possible to chat, face to face, with someone on the other side of the world with the click of a button? Who would have thought that on a tiny telephone you could write little notes to other people and they could read them instantly? My grandparents sure didn't. Suddenly, the world doesn't seem quite as large and quite as inaccessible as it used to be. New technology is amazing in the way that it can allow people to communicate globally, quickly, and easily. Everything I can think of can now be done on a computer. You can pay bills, order food, order clothes, and basically do anything that you want or need to do. If you need a quick recipe for dinner, or an easy explanation about basically anything, a quick type into an internet search engine and thousands of different answers pop up. It has made our every day lives increasingly easy.

There are 870 million cars worldwide today, and with cars becoming a necessity that number is ever-increasing. The amount of negative C02 emissions from one car per year is about 3.5 tons. Cars however, are just one example of technology that has a nega-

---

[59] My essay was written in the style of a pro/con essay. I have two sets of pros and cons and the first set is tied together with this signal phrase as is the second. I set-up my essay so that it had a con followed by a pro, with a small intro at the beginning of the essay and a concluding paragraph at the end.

tive effect on our environment. Another example is recycling old gadgets. Every person that I know has his/her own computer, TV, and/or other technological devices and with this high volume comes high waste.[60] Because of chemicals found in some gadgets, they are increasingly hard to dispose of, which causes a huge environmental threat. New technologically-advanced drilling and mining tools that maximize the amount of natural substances taken from the earth are also a problem. Many of these resources are in limited supply as it is, and these newly invented tools pose a danger of extinction to these resources. The "natural supplies" that we have on the earth are not endless and without many of them human life as we know it would change dramatically. As seen in *Avatar*,[61] industrialization and the use of technologically advanced systems do not always prove positive for the environment and surrounding people.

On the other hand, technology has done wonders for the world[62]; heart transplants, brain surgery, and blood transfusions are all examples of medical miracles that have come about because of the advancement of technology. Millions of people survive each year that otherwise wouldn't, thanks to these advancements. I know many people in my own life that are diagnosed with cancer each year but are helped by chemotherapy treatments. The list of technological/medical miracles stretches far and wide, and if you were to ask anyone in my community if they knew someone that has been saved or helped due to new technology, nearly everyone would answer "yes." Medicine is a positive advance of technology. A mere fifty years ago if someone in our community was diagnosed with measles they would get extremely sick and potentially

---

60 In the past few years the government has gotten better about what old gadgets get sent to landfill sites, but with computers taking 1700 years to decompose it is nearly impossible to truly get rid of your old machines.

61 *Avatar* is a movie that came out in 2009. It is about a richly-forested planet that the human race enters because it holds a valuable substance. There are extreme parallels between the movie and the industrialization of present day. Also, on our trip to Alberta it was referenced by one of the "go-betweens" for an oil company and the local communities.

62 Here is another signal phrase which eases the con argument into the pro argument.

die. However, with the vaccine now given to children, measles is nearly extinct where we live. New technology in medicine saves millions of lives each year, and cures everything from the common cold to heart problems. Without this new technology many people that I know wouldn't be here right now, and that is why it is important to continue to advance our technological capacity.

To me, technology will always be viewed as a double-headed spear.[63] While technology does cause great things it is also starting to change how our human race interacts with one another. Everything from entertainment to business is changing in ways that could be viewed as both bad and good. For thousands of years, people adapted and changed their lifestyles and I think that we are continuing to have to do that in relation to technology. Humankind is becoming completely dependant on technology in every aspect of life and while that isn't necessarily a bad thing, it is a complete change. We have become so immersed in this tidal wave that it is impossible to resist, so we must adapt our lifestyles. However, we must fight so that we do not lose our interpersonal skills or our environment in the process. In one hundred years we will see a dramatic change in human interactions compared to today's world and previous years and it is up to us whether we will sink or swim.

---

[63] This analogy was presented to us in Fort McKay by an oil company representative and I think that it explains what technology does for the world. When the oil representative used this analogy she was referring to how digging oil from the land was great economically speaking but it wasn't great in terms of the earth and the communities surrounding the oilsands.

12

Sustaining 21st century communities
Peter Gibson

The primary concern for a community should be sustainability.[64] Communities have many responsibilities in regard to the physical environment in which we live. Our collective attitudes and daily actions should reflect a desire to protect, grow, and improve the environment for future generations. It is important to examine how drinking water, food, natural habitats, and environmental planning are responsibilities that belong to a community.

A community must supply healthy drinking water for its population.[65] The sources of this water (lakes, rivers, wells, glaciers, etcetera) must be kept clean and free of human-made structures and industries. The community of Fort McKay, Alberta has not sustained its water supply. The Athabasca River was once a source of drinking water for the people of this First Nations reserve until the oil industry polluted the river. The people in the community tried to fight these companies, but they were overpowered. I talked

64 From the onset, I am clearly defining my chosen topic.

65 I present my information in a logical sequence and I use my topic sentences to signal this order.

to an elder who said that when she was a child her father told her that if the companies continued to drill for oil they would not be able to drink from the river. He was right. At the Elders Centre they get their water delivered on a monthly basis. "The water crisis" is becoming a major concern for many countries. We see that some countries take their water for granted, while others do not have access to water.

Healthy foods are essential for our survival. Sustainable forms of agriculture and fishing must be established. If we continue to pollute the environment there will be no room for food development. In Fort McKay the oil industry has effectively reduced the trapping and fishing that was once part of the culture. Talking with people in the community, I learned that where there was once an abundance of animals, few can survive in the environment now. It is necessary to have a continual supply of food for the community.

The natural habitats that we enjoy should be preserved because they serve as natural habitats for many animals, give us clean air, and are great places to enjoy nature. As a child, I remember going camping, going on hikes, and exploring the wilderness. These experiences served not only as ways to have fun, but they also taught me the importance of the environment around me.[66] A lot of communities have significant sites where families have visited as tradition. In Fort McKay, this place is Moose Lake. Families would visit Moose Lake to learn how to trap, fish, and live off the land. The oil industry threatens to destroy traditional access routes to this heritage site. Natural habitats such as green spaces are not limited to natural ecosystems, but can also be created by people. Parks and reforestation should be considered as important environmental developments in a community.

There are three ways that communities can work collectively toward their environmental responsibilities. Firstly, waste removal is something we should be conscious of in our communities. Recycling programs, composting, and sewage treatment are just some of

---

[66] I used a personal anecdote to connect with my learning in Fort McKay. This allows readers to think about their own experiences in natural habitats.

the ways we can ensure that we have a healthy environment. Secondly, responsibility within a community can also mean incorporating new transportation systems to avoid high levels of greenhouse gas emissions. Public transit could become so efficient that no one would have to own a vehicle. The concept of conserving on fuel consumption is foreign to many. Thirdly, renewable forms of energy and innovative technology are starting to be used more and more. Local governments can strategically plan to switch to wind turbines, solar panels, and electric cars.

Communities also have responsibilities surrounding social environments. The people in the community should have a healthy relationship with the industry. In Alberta, Rod Hyde told me that the oil companies are examining their environmental standards because this is a necessity. However, it could be argued that they are neglecting the people in the community. It is true that they are putting money into the schools, the Elders Centre, the Wellness Centre, and this is great. They should have to give back for all that they are taking away. The oil companies must monitor the social impact they have had on the community and work with the people to ensure they are functioning together.

Communities should assume responsibility in educating their youth about the importance of sustainability and the environment. Lessons can be learned from past generations and must be considered by young people.[67] While visiting a Métis trapper named Tommy, I heard him talk about how a lot of his knowledge had come from the people before him. His family had taught him how to trap, how to be an outdoors man. There is much we can learn from the people who had a sustainable lifestyle and who lived off the land by trapping and fishing.

Local governments must have leaders who are willing to take action and improve their community designs and planning. Dorothy MacDonald, a former chief in Fort McKay stood up for her people. She fought the oil industry because they were harming the

[67] This reminds me of listening to the elders speak and how young people in the community don't automatically respect their elders.

land. The chief wanted the best for her community and this is the kind of mindset everyone needs to have. Sustainable communities begin with the actions of people in the community and they extend to the surrounding industries.

In many communities, industry threatens to overshadow[68] environmental concern. The concerns that people have for the environment are gradually influenced by the industry. In many cases, people may feel like there is nothing that they can do to improve or protect the environment. One elder in Fort McKay told me that from his point of view only the industry had responsibilities for the environment. Citizens should not feel so overwhelmed by the destruction the industry is causing that they feel helpless. We can work together to come up with new forms of energy and new technologies that do not harm the industry or the community. *Everybody* has responsibilities when it comes to their physical and social environment. The common mindset that money is a number one priority is a frightening reality in our world today. Instead, we must make environmental responsibility within our communities a top priority.

[68] The word overshadow is powerful because it describes the way industry can have an impact on society. This word is appropriate because I think industry affects the community gradually.

13

The pedagogy of individual inquiry questions

Steven Van Zoost, PhD

First, a story: I didn't see it coming—this book, I mean. I didn't plan for my students to write this book, or produce a documentary, or co-write sponsorship letters using a wiki in a Moodle environment. I didn't plan (or even dream) to go to northern Alberta in the dead of winter. Trust me. It was the students who inspired this project, not me.

Now, a confession: I should have seen it coming—this project, I mean. The students involved in this Youth Inquiry Project were used to working with individualized inquiry questions within our classroom. It was not as if these students imagined this book without prior experience in asking, exploring, and writing about their own questions of the world. In fact, using inquiry questions was a guiding pedagogical structure to their Grade 12 Advanced English Language Arts course design.

In September, we conducted an author study. We had an in-depth look at the writing of Alden Nowlan who was born and raised in the community of Stanley, a twenty minute drive from our high school. We read a common text (a biography of Nowlan) and a collection of his writing that we shared. Each student developed his or her own inquiry question about Nowlan's body of work. One student was interested in looking at the role of rural imagery in his writing, especially as the imagery might be particular to Hants County. Another student was interested in thinking about how Nowlan's exposure to religion as a child played out in his writing. While we read and discussed Nowlan's work in class, each student was thinking, recording, and eventually writing about a different focus of Nowlan's work.

In October, the focus of our class was a particular issue: women's rights. We read a common fictional text concerning women's rights in Afghanistan. The students also had a common assignment to interview a female family member or community member about what it is like to be a woman living in Hants County. A third common experience was that we interviewed Casey Brown, the principal of Fort McKay School in Alberta about what it is like to be a woman living and working in a First Nations community surrounded by the oilsands industry. Regardless of text or experience, throughout the month of October, each student was pursuing a self-designed question about women's rights.

In November, our class focus was an historical focus about the Holocaust. While we shared common texts, the students also chose individual texts about the Holocaust. Each student developed their own inquiry question that they considered throughout the month. One student was interested in how the Holocaust could have occurred. Another student was interested in the role of the bystander during the Holocaust and what can be learned about citizenship in today's world.

<table>
<tr><th colspan="5">2009-2010 course design organized by units of study</th></tr>
<tr><td>September</td><td>October</td><td>November</td><td>December</td><td>January</td></tr>
<tr><td>Author Study: Alden Nowlan</td><td>Issue: Women's Rights</td><td>Historical Exploration: The Holocaust</td><td>Major Text: Othello</td><td rowspan="2">Theme: 21st Century Communities</td></tr>
<tr><td colspan="2">Writing Workshop (once a week)</td><td colspan="2">Youth Inquiry Project (once a week)</td></tr>
</table>

I am stressing these experiences because I want to point out how it is possible to structure individual student inquiries in a variety of ways. A common author, issue, event, or text can be used to frame a unit of study for the entire class while allowing for individual student interests to be pursued. It is essential to help young people become equipped with the skills needed to raise and pursue their own questions and concerns about the world. In the twenty-first century, teaching English Language Arts is less about telling students dominant and common interpretations of a novel or play that is read by every student in the class and more about teaching young people how to unlearn their certainty about the world. This can be daunting for students and teachers alike.

In October, after the students spoke with Casey Brown about women's rights on a speaker-phone, the class wanted to learn more about Fort McKay. This was the moment where my flexibility faced-off with my need to be organized and planned. In my original course design, January was planned to explore the issue of 21st century communication (a topic I had chosen without much student input). However, in September, I invited students to put forward other ideas for January. I had planned flexibility into the course design. "Come back on Monday and tell me why you want to learn more about this community," was all I was willing to commit after that fateful phone conversation with Casey Brown.

On Monday, I was convinced. I also knew that I had to be optimistic or I risked being dismissed by my students. Young people are incredibly optimistic about the world and it has been my experience that they have no use for people who are not optimistic about themselves, their futures, and the world. As one parent told me, "These kids think that the sky is the limit." Fortunately, my nature is largely optimistic, although my experience made me wary of the financial hurdles of getting to see Fort McKay.

When I used individual inquiry questions in my classroom, my role as the teacher changed: I needed to follow students' interests and at the same time, help students think through these same interests. For example, Garrett's original question was, "What is a community?" His definition essay was intended to be a conceptual overview for this book and so the question evolved to, "What is a community in the 21st century?" However, in discussion with Garrett (via email and face-to-face), we both came to realize that his question was limiting because it was a "closed" question, suggesting that there was only one "right" answer. For each of the student's original inquiry questions, I offered (on-line) two or three re-phrased options that prompted further thinking. In class, I met with each student to discuss how to focus their inquiry question or to increase the scope of their question. My role as the teacher was to help young people think about the kinds of questions that they deemed worthwhile asking about their own communities in rural Nova Scotia as well as about other communities such as Fort McKay. This was delicate work. I did not want to impose my thinking or veer students away from their own interest. My most successful strategy was to offer more than one suggestion. My second best strategy was to offer a series of contradictory suggestions. Garrett's question changed to become a more "open-ended" question: What does the word "community" mean in the 21st century?

Inquiry-based learning is nothing new in the world of education. Now, in the 21st century, educators need to take-up pedagogical stances that engage young people in schools, in their own learning, and in their own lives. Passive learning is passé; student engagement is the future to keeping students interested in coming to school. Watching the students involved in this Youth Inquiry Project, I can attest to their high level of engagement as well as their increased respect for their own learning processes. The thinking projects that were initiated by 17 and 18 year old students in this anthology remind me again not to confuse intelligence with experience. Young people are interested in challenging issues and need opportunities to use questions to learn.

Finally, a hope: I wish for more questions—for you, I mean. My intent is that this book will raise questions about education, young people, and today's world and that you, like me, will value young people as vital members of our communities.

Questions to Learn: A Youth Inquiry Project Documentary

Questions to Learn: A Youth Inquiry Project follows the journey of the Advanced English 12 class at Avon View High School (2009-2010) featured in this book as they initiate this project designed around individual inquiry questions. The documentary explains how the idea for the project began, what kinds of questions interested the students, and how the inquiry questions shaped their thinking. The project involved visiting Fort McKay School, Alberta to meet Principal Casey Brown.

Producers: Steven Van Zoost, Duncan Armour, Peter Gibson

Featuring music from A.S.T. (Alice Stops Time)
http://www.myspace.com/stoptimealice

Length: 13 minutes, 24 seconds

Available from www.stevenvanzoost.com

Itinerary: Youth Inquiry Project
January 2010

January 4-14

- Individual inquiry questions about 21st Century communities confirmed
- Book Chapter planning and writing: structure, outlines, principal ideas, tone, inquiry/thinking/reflection pieces
- Preparation of presentations to Fort McKay school
- Documentary structure planning and initial footage filmed

January 15, Friday

- Flight From Halifax to Fort McMurray:
- Shuttle to hotel in Fort McMurray: Nomad Inn

January 16, Saturday

- Breakfast at Hotel
- Oilsands Discovery Centre 9:30 am – 12:15 pm
- Lunch at A & W 12:45 pm – 1:45 pm
- Swimming at YMCA 2:30 pm – 4:30 pm
- Supper at Boston Pizza (Timberlea) 5:30 pm – 7:00 pm
- Oil Baron's Hockey Game 7:30 pm – 10:00 pm
- Group debriefing session, individual reflection time, documentary filming

January 17, Sunday

- Breakfast at Hotel
- Anzac Trapline with Tom Bourque 10:00 am – 4:30 pm
  · Tobogganing
  · Métis Trapper session
  · Visit Cabin and Trapline, Chili lunch
- Supper at Moxie's 5:30 pm – 7:00 pm
- Group debriefing session, individual reflection time, documentary filming

January 18, Monday

- Breakfast at Hotel
- Drive to Fort McKay, passing Suncor and Syncrude
- Arrive at Fort McKay School 8:30 am
  · Introductions
- Fort McKay School Morning Routine 8:55 am – 9:30 am
- Presentation 9:30 am – 12:00
  · Rod Hyde – community history
  · Dayle Hyde – growing up in Fort McKay
- Lunch – Bag Lunch from Staff 12:00 – 1:00 pm
- Classroom Presentations 1:00 pm – 3:30 pm
  · Small Groups with Nova Scotia students
- Return to Fort McMurray 4:00 pm
- Supper at Montana's 5:30 pm – 6:45 pm
- Group debriefing session, individual reflection time, documentary filming

January 19, Tuesday

- Breakfast at Hotel
- Arrive at Fort McKay School 8:30 am
- FMS Morning Routine 8:55 am – 9:30 am
- Cross Country Ski Workshop 9:30 am – 11:00 am
- Classroom Visits 11:00 am – 11:45 am
- Lunch with Elders at new centre 12:00 pm – 1:00 pm
- Visit with Elders 1:00 pm – 3:00 pm
  · How things have changed/impact of industry
  · Past/present/future
  · Life of a trapper
- Daycare Visit 3:00 pm – 3:30 pm
- Wellness Centre Visit 4:00 pm – 5:00 pm
- Supper at Wellness Centre 5:00 pm – 6:00 pm
- Family Night at Fort McKay School 6:00 pm – 7:30 pm
- Return to Fort McMurray 7:30 pm
- Group debriefing session, individual reflection time, prepare for return

January 20, Wednesday

- EARLY Flight from Fort McMurray to Halifax

January 21-25

- Finalization of book for publication
- Editing and production of documentary
- Contact with sponsors and media

Photo
January 2010

www.ingramcontent.com/pod-product-compliance
Ingram Content Group UK Ltd.
Pitfield, Milton Keynes, MK11 3LW, UK
UKHW041918190726
13854UKWH00003B/1310